IT BLOOMS AMONGST THE ASHES

IT BLOOMS AMONGST THE ASHES

NOVELLA BEX

Novella Bex

Contents

	Dedication	viii
1.	Introduction	1
	1 The Mother of all Fears	2
	State Of Nihility	3
	Doom Room	4
	Dark Showers	6
	Atonement	8
	Stone Flower	9
	Monsters And Men	10
	Visitors	12
	Worth Saving	13
	Black Velvet	14
	Paper Doll	16
	Cello	17

Rain That Never Comes	18
Mirror Mirror	19
II The Reparation	22
Smile	23
Concealer	24
Lifeguard	25
Domain	26
Feel Me	27
Discover Me In Prayer	28
Internalize	29
Dark Lullaby	30
Quicksand	31
All Waves Crash	32
Soul To Keep	33
Letter In The Clouds	34
Destroy Me Not	36
III The Safety of Love	37
The Fall	38
Strong Tides	40
Adoration	41
Battlefield	42

True Sight	43
Loved In A Look	45
Page Turner	46
Escape Into Me	47
Unmatched Blossoms	48
Sweetness	49
A Different Love	50
Breakfast Muse	51
Soul Mate	52
Progression In Bloom	53
About The Author	55

Dedicated to the silence that speaks volumes.

Copyright © 2020 by Novella Bex

All rights reserved. No part of this book may be reproduced in any manner whatsoever without written permission except in the case of brief quotations embodied in critical articles and reviews.

Cover Illustrator: istock.com/victor_tongdee
Book Illustrator: fiverr.com/jeffreyzico

First Printing, 2020

Introduction

She smiled amidst her nightmares and forged war for her soul.

At times conflicted in her spirit, her flaws often were exposed.

The wilting of her petals brought new meaning for the Sun
She bloomed through hell and fury; her thoughts forced to come undone

For her to build the garden she hadn't realized she'd become.

I

The Mother of all Fears

Putrid is the soul that cleanses with the tears of others.

State of Nihility

I am the girl that is used to service others.

My hair lays plain where my clothes once remained and untouched by the words they utter.

My lips press firmly to hold prisoner the pain that my body wishes to cry.

Your hands round my neck as you force your erect in between my young bruised thighs.

I look to your face for remorse or distaste for the mess you have made out of me

But you smile all the while immersed in the wiles of a man that seeks evil need.

My longing for the child that blew dandelions on the days with the bluest of skies

But now feels as lost and abandoned as the tears that no longer flow from her eyes.

Doom Room

My words flew out before I could hold them back and your face was unleashed.

Fear trembled my body and there I stood paralyzed from it.

You hurl toward me lifting me up and over your shoulder.

Your nails deep into my sides as your gait quickens toward the room.

That room.

My hands search for anything to grasp, perhaps another hand will appear for me to hold onto.

I scrape lines down the walls of my fate.

It is right before where I gain my mightiest of grips on the corners of Doom.

Paint and wood make their way under my nails and my fingers begin to bleed.

One hard tug and though my hold stays strong, what was held becomes undone.

Another failed attempt.

Dark Showers

Dark showers hold a dark power

Here rivers flow down my cheeks and are camouflaged
against the iridescent pour
Here I sit, knees to chest yearning to be washed of your sin
that has stained my skin

How deceitful this place that promises cleansing when no
matter the harsh scrub, I am never clean.

Atonement

My eyes force their way open to meet yours. Deep shades of black with two auburn spots. I see such empathy that washes over your face. You lift me up and handle me with such fragility.

I fade.

I awake to you holding me in the water. You wash my body so gently. The way your hands move across my skin; I am mesmerized by your tenderness. You wash the hurt from between me and wrap it with care.

Once again your eyes meet my surprise and you look directly into my soul and hold it. I am captivated by your compassion to repair me.

Is this the same beast that did this to me?

Why repair what you have broken?

Or is it your own broken you wish to make whole again?

Stone Flower

She works.
She prays.
She knows her fate, but still her smile stays on her face.
I know this girl. She dreams big dreams. She walks as though nothing's happening.
But when she leaves that school escape, she'll go back home to his dark place and she'll give
and give,
and give herself,
and she'll cry her silent cry for help
But she knows
She only cries alone.
There was a man who made her feel beyond the gleam of sex appeal. He held her heart and kept it safe, but she knew she'd run and so she breaks
His heart to feel an inch of pain of what she felt from her past shame.
And he tried
and tried
to make her see, that this Love was really happening.
But she knows.
Her heart is made of Stone.

Monsters and Men

I saw you through my welled-up eyes. He was penetrating my innocence and you stood there.
You stood there in the doorway with that face of sorrow.
Why are you sorrowful if you will not speak light into this dark room?
He tears into my body and still you stand and watch.
You exit; you with head down as you pull that shield of denial over your eyes.
Yes, hold your head down with shame, for I see that you were the real monster in my darkness.

Visitors

Their hands are rough like the pads of homeless feet.
The grips feel familiar.
The smell of their sweat weighs on me and assists the hold.
They fill me with their filth.
They get off on my cries.

Can't you see? You cannot defile me into Oblivion, for I am already here.

Worth Saving

Do you hear me?
Your eyes tell me you do.
Do you hear the screaming beneath this blanket of silence?
Read my eyes.
The screams paint a ransom note scarred across my body.
Why am I not worth saving to you?

Black Velvet

That night was something I felt, a deep ravine of a scene.
I stood before you the girl you wished you could be.
My skin was tan, hair long, luscious and wild like the best of my dreams.
But you had something in for me, your eyes reflected only jealousy.
His words brought that part of you that was clear through the tipsy you pretended to be.

It was for you that I wept.
I froze as he poured the poison that smelt of the devils' breath.
My own sweat and tears flowed down my neck, the hairs stood erect.
This cannot be my end said my head, but it was my heart that leapt.
It fell into the place where the young girls are kept.
The girl dressed in black velvet that made her pelt wet.
Will I be met with mercy? Will their minds change?
Will they yell cut, will the scenes change sets?

Still I stand with a fate soon to be met.

I close my eyes and wish for a way.
A way for you to love me in the light despite this terrible shade.
I opened to find your eyes were not in a haze, but yet surprisingly vivid; the reflection was me ablaze.
My cries rang out like the waves that he craved.
You both watched my pain till my ashes made my grave.

That night I watched your soul leave, something I hoped had stayed.
I continue to this day to do the only thing I believe that can save you despite the flames that still remain.

I pray.

Paper Doll

There was not a stitch on me I had made myself.
You are intertwined into every fiber of my being.
Your chosen colors.
Your chosen buckles and latches.
The tie around my neck that hid
the hands that made me submit.

I am the face of your best collection.
But will they buy it?

Cello

My tears bleed on the bow. It saturates the strings with a sound so deafening to the soul that it drowns out the cries until there is calm.
And then I bleed again.

Rain that Never Comes

I pray for rain.
I bleed your sin onto the floor.
My thoughts no longer reside here, as I turn numb.
It is by choice to feel nothing.
No pain.
No joy.
No hurt.
No Love.
I am but crimson that stains the white between the tiles.

Mirror Mirror

I pull the fabric from the mirror and breathe deeply. It has been a long time since I have seen this reflection in such darkness. My heart beats as if in a race. I close my eyes and hear its steady pumping and await the sound that starts the reel, I feel your hot breath next to my ear. "Watch yourself", you whisper. I want you to watch yourself cry; WATCH!" My eyes fly open and the memory forms again.
I Watch as you force the wet from my eyes.
I Watch myself yearning for you to take my life like the innocence you have already stolen many times before.
I Watch as my body cringes, the daily trigger of such unbearable pain.
I Watch as my tears fall to the carpet below And I Watch your look of complete satisfaction.
Over and Over
Day after Day
I watched like you commanded me.
Until that day I no longer harbored any tears to shed. Till I no longer held any love for myself to fight.
That is the day I saw you shine your red light. I angered the beast in you. What you desired I no longer produced.
Your eyes were unlike anything I had ever seen that day.

Did you know what you were doing? I want to believe that you didn't. I want to believe in so much good in you despite it all.

I remember my disbelief. I remember screaming and only silence escaping me. That rage you yielded with such conviction. I remember the trail to where you left me; my own crimson forming my mirror once again against that tile.

I close my eyes now full of my own rage.
How you have affected everything I hold close.
How every decision to not love deeply came from you.
How every scar I bear is inflamed with your guilt.

I open my eyes and yield my own steel. The scream I never got to have.
The scream that shatters you.
My light is no longer afraid of your Dark mirrors
It is your turn to watch now
Watch me Triumph
Watch me forgive you

II

The Reparation

Search for the parts of yourself that still hide and call them out. Reach for them before they are lost forever.

Smile

Through the turmoil within you, still you wear it. You believe this to be one of your greatest masks, but what lies behind it, stands ready, like an army.

The sound of angst pushes against the curves of the mouth. Waiting with weaponry that would pierce even the bravest of warriors.

HOLD.... and lift.
We shall fight another day.

Concealer

Hide your subtle cracks and they just might not see how much glue you used to piece yourself together.

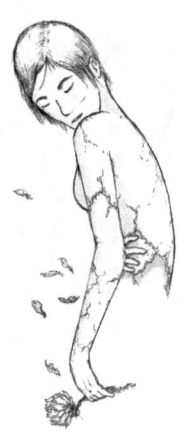

Lifeguard

Stay close sweet Love, for my hands have fought off bigger demons than you can imagine.

I will protect you.

Domain

    I am filled and immerse in the ecstasy. Why have I fallen for the very thing that ruined me? The very thing I hold hatred for? What twisted perception have I grown accustomed to?

    The touch sends me on a trip the eyes could never voyage. I block the heart and urge the head to rule. This is my kingdom. Here I sit untouchable. They dare not rise above the hairline of my power or risk the ash that will remain of them.

Feel Me

Immerse in my Dreamaverse

Discover Me in Prayer

I found you.
I thought you had forgotten me. I thought you were only watching; testing me, but I found you.
Beneath the labored breaths
Beneath the hands that choked my cries
The eyes staring back at me in the mirror
I prayed and I found you.

Internalize

I sit here in the circle of confessions. How does one speak of such vile things to complete strangers? How am I to heal this way amongst the other broken?

I contemplate if these methods do more harm than help but still I sit and listen.

I listen to the man that bore the print of an angered father. I listen to the young mother speak of her abusive relationship through a cracked voice. I listen to the woman who suffered through her breaking point and afflicted self-harm.

I listen and I hurt for them.

I hurt for me.

My turn comes and I stare at curious faces. My first time to my twenty-first time here and still I say all that my heart can manage..."pass"

Will I ever get it out?

Dark Lullaby

Late Night. Sleep Tight. Small words, though wise. I see you, for who you are. I adore thee
I remember you. You brought light to my Heart. There's no fooling a fool, sing to me like that Lark.
Scream the sweet lullaby, breathe that Vanilla sky; through this pain I shall cry till these memories die.
Through the thickness within, I tried again and again to bring you back to my end of ends.
I remember you. You sought grasp of my soul. There's no Peace for the weak, when its told and retold
Hang your head with much shame, stop those faux polish games I believe in your good, shake that could and be should
I remember your scares, those sleepless nights just because. You cried, you cried in your dreams, those words not so foreseen.
Late Night, when darkness shines through; you ache from the pain you once knew
The fire beneath your scars, the feelings not forgot
You cry for the girl that pulled through. She is you.
Late night, sleep tight, small words, though wise. I see you, for who you are I adore thee.

Quicksand

Why have I not detached from you?
You pull me into you and cloak me with a type of surrounding I could never escape.

Even when provided the rope to which I can swing across you;
my choice remains.
I let go...and let you.

All Waves Crash

I lose balance and am enveloped by you; pulling me under.
Do you have no mercy for the unstable as you thrash me around under your skin?
I fight tirelessly to escape you, yet you hold me still and force me to recognize defeat.

I let go and you allow me to rise to the surface of my fear.

I awake with the sun upon my face and inhale what was once lost.
I float amidst your lesson and realize that in order to ride the wave, I must first endure the fall.

Soul to Keep

In the days I was weak, you robbed of me my mind.
I sought shelter with a priest and in the words of the wise.
I pondered in thought should I fight or shall I die.
So I fought with my fists
but you broke my hands.
Then I fought with my strength
and you shattered my bones
So I'll fight with my heart, so prepare
your defeat, for this soul of mine you will never own

Letter in the Clouds

I feel your hurt Dark Cloud. I hear of your pain.
At times we long for cleansing in this life that brands us with stains.
The stains that assist our swaddle of dark, despite our thrashing to become free. Will you ever be healed, you ask.
Will I ever be Me?

Your pen tells the world of your cuts, but the eyes are mere bruised.
True sight comes from a release of the old and embrace for the new.
I cried in my dark shower for you amid my own dark hues.
No stranger to longing for relief but what I found was a Muse.
Do we circle the drain with our sorrows or face our own truth?

I ask you. Are you prepared for the vision that I see for you?
That you will someday draw the clouds of your past without all the sorrows accrued? I can tell you this from my experiences so listen closely for this truth
One day you will speak of that moment with tears you

have cried, release the yell to the wind and open your eyes to
find
no dark clouds lurk above you;
only the clearest of skies.

Destroy Me Not

You destroyed my body only to reveal my soul.
It takes heart to overcome, to persevere.
Destructive hands remain idle when there is no weak to prey on.

III

The Safety of Love

If simple words are able to cripple a spirit, imagine how powerful a great Love can repair the soul.

The Fall

Meet me at the cliff young girl.

Let us walk to the edge of this part of you made up of the years of tears.
Feel the wind on your face, feel the sound in your ears.
Spread your arms out wide; let go right now, right here.

Fall against the breeze.
I promise this part of you, you were meant to leave.
Feel the pile of leaves at your back, let your heart be at ease.
We fall to be caught; caught up in Happy.

Strong Tides

My expedition halts between two lighthouses that both beacon me toward safety.
What if I don't make it to either?
What if I become but ruins amongst the rock that guard their own sanctuary?
Perhaps it is them that need safeguard from me, a wayward voyager.

Adoration

I love the part of you that hides from the part of me.

Battlefield

I'm in love with the realization that a great love can change your life. Make you turn on that part of you that claims you don't deserve it.
Make you put on the crimson paint and fight to the death for it yelling against the sounds of the drums...Victory is mine!
Even when you awake to what looks like defeat.
You smile.
What a glorious death.

True Sight

My fierce encounter with Love came like a storm not predicted. I was in denial until it showed itself as blatantly as crying in front of that mirror.

How barren and completely exposed it made me. His eyes found the part of me I hadn't even searched for nor I knew existed.

I was completely enamored by his splendor and what a humble splendor he was. His eyes hung onto you like a man lost at sea clinging to any piece of his wreckage. I jumped in. I had a need to save him. A need to reach out and show him, no man drowns among those that refuse to sink.

His beauty shines beyond any physical form. I breathe him in. I feel undeserving of such Love. My belief was always that I held control over my heart, but tis the mind that tells the truth of how that is never so. It whispers its spoken word to me like the wind whistles through the trees. I was selective to not hear it, but it forces its way upon my ears, and I am faced with the irrevocable truth of how I feel.

God has painted my spirit with the colors of him. How I love to love him. How I love to create all the colors of him inside my world. But I cannot take credit for this Art. I am simply a vessel for what it makes me. How much better it makes me. I am merely the paint, the wooden brush, but tis Love that is the only canvas for such vision.

My brush misses the cup and I touch my scarred eyes as a sigh fills me. It seems Love has blinded me.

Loved In a Look

The curve of his smile touches the creases around his eyes and I am lost in him.
How his smile melts me like the Tuscan sun in the heart of summer.

I feel as though I sway amongst the cypress when he looks at me.

I feel warmth.
I feel free.
I feel Loved.

Page Turner

Are you real?

I touch your face searching for the fold to which I can strip away to reveal who you really are but find no unturned pages.

It appears you are a first edition.

Escape into Me

Time and a place, I find myself caught up in the chase.
You know you have my heart Love; you shine light in my darkest of place
Feeling fine, with your kisses down my spine.
The very taste of your affection has me sprung outside the lines.
But I want your mind
Far past the depths of internal decline.
Where you fear your reflection, where your dark rules over your light
And Love, that's ok, for I got the cure for your mental embrace; just lay here with me in the moment and let me take it away.

Unmatched Blossoms

There would be no me without you.

Your words hit my soul like the sun hits the flower when the day is new.

Your touch held my breath in ways only my heart felt.
I quiver from the thought of the first time you made me melt.

You reached in and took the feelings I had always kept at bay.
Till it was no longer your touch I longed for; it was your love that I craved.

Did I dream your feelings up? Was any of it true?
I know this flower will never be what you desire,
but there would be no me without you.

Thank you

Sweetness

Love me like the tongue loves the truffle.

A Different Love

Be the kind of Love that makes them feel strong and weak at the knees.

Breakfast Muse

Your voice melts over me and I disperse like butter atop fresh biscuits.
The air is sweet when you approach me. I stand frozen as to not shutter as you move closer. Heaven help me for I may unravel right here amidst the public.

Why do you satisfy my heart like you satisfy my eyes? Your tranquil persona is the essence of how every morning should start, fresh and breathing life into me.

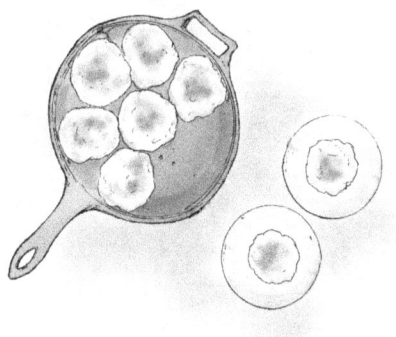

Soul Mate

It was a pain so crippling I felt I may collapse and be
buried in that red chair. You place your hand on my arm with
your head down in prayer whispering your sweet poetry to
God to bring me relief.
It ceases and I look at you, consumed in prayer and I knew
right then and there
I was in Love with the sight of your soul.

Progression in Bloom

Pick up the pieces of the wreckage to form your whole again.
The pieces may have faded and the corners tattered, not quite a fit for its original form.
Your portrait no longer the same, but nonetheless Beautiful.
Does the flower still bloom, you ask, if no one sees her pick herself up?

A beautiful form may graze his hands against your petals now.
Welcome this touch, as it is finally your own choice to do so.
Close your eyes and sway in and out of love.
You may hold his hands to discover the harshness of their surface for he holds you despite the thorns that were too much for you to bear.
You will weep at times asking, Will I ever get back what was taken?
Will I ever see worth in myself? Have I lost the taste for happiness?

Years later the memory will still walk through your garden

with its dirty boots. Leaving behind the mud on your outstretched blooms that worked so hard to reach the sun.
Fear not for the sun shall kiss your cheek again and play for you its sweet sound that will bring joy to your soul.
That feeling is the sun's poetry to the flower; always encouraging it to open its beauty to his.
Will you have found peace amid this life at last?
Has the flower been spoken for?

The raw truth is, the aftermath will weigh like debris from a storm that took no prisoners and often you will be exposed as an open book.
Work to be seen for what you are, not what has happened to you.

Forgiveness is not a task without trial but by giving it fully there is hope yet still for all the Flowers that bloomed in hell.

Novella Bex is an American poet, writer, photographer, and author of,
It Blooms Amongst the Ashes,
An honest and raw portrayal of the inner turmoil from a young girl colliding with the triumph of a woman.

Novella's first creative beginnings were that in black and white photography as a hope to capture the raw, candid beauty of people and the world around her. From there her sense of release came in the form of writing out her memories with the same exposed visual as the photos she captured.

"If I can reach even one soul and pull them through that suffering to a place of refuge and peace, I have fulfilled my purpose; and all good books have purpose; even the ones of ourselves we are often too afraid to read."

Novella Bex can be followed on her website *novellabex.com* and social media, instagram account *@novellabex* for more writing and visual works.

www.ingramcontent.com/pod-product-compliance
Lightning Source LLC
Chambersburg PA
CBHW071320080526
44587CB00018B/3299